SHADES OF A
RAMADHAN
1443AH

BINT IBRAHIM

Published in Nigeria by
Mutiah Badruddeen Publishers

Printed by
LawpatNG Brands
www.lawpatng.com
@lawpatng

when I finally had a copy, intending to glance through and wait for 1st Ramadhan before taking the poems piecemeal, I could not resist the urge to keep flipping the pages. Before I knew it I was at the end of the book. The poems never get old and I can't wait to open the pages again to start afresh even after Ramadhan. It really went a long way in being a worthy companion during that sacred month. The thought of another SOAR to move together with on a daily basis this Ramadhan makes the wait more intensifying.

Ibrahim Majidadi Esq

My first impression of SOAR is that it's beautiful. Upon further perusal, I see more beauty evolving and I am struck by how appropriate it is. Just what I need...reminders that evoke thoughts and actions. Unique. A refreshingly simple tool to enhance your ibaadat yet the poems are thought provokingly poignant. I pray that the benefit of this book does not elude us both. JazaakumuLlahu khairan for a wonderful effort. Baraaka Llahu feek.

Fatima Omoyele
Founder, Fitrah Schools

About the shades of Ramadhan (SOAR). My reaction right now is "hmm". Subhanallah. Barakallahu feeki ukhtii jameelah. I shed tears at some point. It really resonates with me. I can't put my words together. Indeed it's a shade of Ramadhan. I've found my companion for the blessed month and I pray it becomes useful to me. Bi'ithni llahi

Karimah Lawal
Founder, Careyscuisine

Purple royal; keeping me in tune with the greatness of the One I serve. Free lessons on Arabic numbers got me going Masha Allah! Day 3 finally got my juices going - whatever is decreed for me will never pass me by!

Adekemi Adisa
General Manager, Organisation Effectiveness and Performance, MTN Nigeria

Alhamdulilah I got S.O.A.R., It's such an awesome reminder, Jazak Allahu khairan. You have "woken up" the writer in me. I seek your permission to use some stanzas in some of my presentations (If u didn't know I'm "Oliver Twist" and will be asking for more.) My words will "scream" like my Voice. Thanks so much sis.

Rekiya Etiko
Educational consultant
C.E.O Naia Educational Consult

Acknowledgments

All thanks and praise is due to Allah.

We seek His help and forgiveness, and we seek refuge in Allah from the evil within ourselves and the consequences of our evil deeds. Whoever Allah guides will never be led astray, and whomever Allah leads astray will never find guidance. I bear witness that there is no God but Allah, alone without any partners, and I bear witness that Muhammad (peace and blessings be upon him) is His servant and His Messenger.

Allah Almighty said, "O you who have faith, fear Allah as it is His right to be feared and do not die except as Muslims" (3:102) And Allah Almighty said, "O people, fear your Lord, who created you from one soul and created from it its mate and dispersed from both of them many men and women. Fear Allah, through whom you ask one another and maintain family ties. Verily, Allah is ever watching over you." (4:1)

And Allah Almighty said, "O you who have faith, fear Allah and speak upright words. He will correct your deeds and forgive your sins. Whoever obeys Allah and His Messenger has won a tremendous victory." (33:70-71)

Verily, the most truthful speech is the Book of Allah, the best guidance is the guidance of Muhammad (peace and blessings be upon him), and the worst of affairs are newly invented matters.

Every newly invented matter is a religious innovation, and every religious innovation is misguidance, and every misguidance is in the Hellfire.

* * * * * * * * * * * *

It's another call to prepare for the blessed month of Ramadhan... and as I always say, there can never be enough of them. You know the story behind these so I won't tell it again.

SOAR is here once more. For Allah. And then For You.

To seek Allah's pleasure, with the hope that sharing this journey will earn His Barakah, bi'ithnillah. And, that it may inspire you to pen down your feelings and experiences of the best month of the year. Pace, Plan, Perfect and Progress. The only things guiding you being the very things you exist for...Ibaadah and Obedience.

Thank you once again for taking up SOAR 1442AH. For those who ordered:
- Because of our relationship (and yes I hassled some of you one-on-one)
- Read reviews and ordered because of that
- For family members that didn't even get a chance to own a copy
- And made them a part of gift boxes,
- And gifted strangers, just because
- And used as corporate gifts
- In support, work colleagues, not of the same faith
- And offered to stock, sell or just be pick-up points.

Jazakallahu khairan.

All praise alone is to Allah.

Copies of SOAR flooded your timelines on Social Media and the feedback was so uplifting. I have shared some on here. These words of admonition gave many of us, myself included, renewed inspiration each day.

For all these people and more, if SOAR moved you enough to make your Ramadhan more reflective and cause you to take action, then this attempt is well worthy insha Allah before our Lord's eyes and I am grateful.

I will be remiss if I didn't make special mention of my Zawj for handling logistics and generally keeping me accountable, my agency Sage Accent (one-man army), Mr Sam and of course my publishers. May Allah bestow His blessings and Rahma on you all. Ameen.

It's time to once again take these pages, these words, and find one more way to earn His pleasure. Please do not forget to spare a prayer for me that the One who owns us all is pleased with my intention, these verses and this effort. Ameen.

May we have the very best Ramadhan yet. Ameen.

May we have homes in Jannah together. Ameen.

Bismillah.

— Bint Ibrahim.
1443AH

SHADES OF A
RAMADHAN
1443AH

As an Expiation

Narrated by Abu Wail from Hudhaifa, who said:

`Umar asked the people, "Who remembers a narration from the Prophet ﷺ *about the affliction?" Hudhaifa said, "I heard the Prophet* ﷺ *saying, 'The affliction of a person in his property, family and neighbors is expiated by his prayers, fasting, and giving in charity ..."*
— Sahih al-Bukhari 1895

.١

now.

i'm back,
again, ya Allah,
never let me stop returning
to you, till you finally come for me;

ya Allah, never let me stop,
for belief stops when one stops
returning to one's Rabb, ya rabb.

.٢

may you find me ready, ya Allah,
in my heart, deeds and thoughts;
when you eventually come for me.

may i be a devout a'bd of yours,
one forgiven, beloved, and guided;
may i never stray from your path,
ya Allah, and may i be loved by you.

.٣

and as i wait, and live;

surround me, ya Allah,
with your sakeenah, sabr, nur,

and do not forsake me, ya Allah,
even for a twinkling of an eye.

ya Allah, let me find who i am again,
let her please you, and never let me let go of her.

.٤

ya Allah, keep me forever grateful,
through pain and tears, grit and survival,
love and doubt, floundering and hope,
faith and faithfulness, always.

for it is the grateful that believes,
whilst the ungrateful despairs
of your mercies and sustenance.

.٥

i'm back,
again,
ya Allah,
ease my affairs, now,
ya Allah, ease my affairs, today,
ease my affairs, tomorrow,
and for ever and ever. amin.

it begins

.١

speechless!

where did the time go?
a blessing returns.
not by any might of ours,
but only by the mercy of the One,
the true One, who everything relies on,
the One we owe all to.

.٢

the time is upon us again,
another day, a fresh start,
an amazing opportunity;
indeed, we are grateful,
to be amongst the chosen;

some of us are here no more,
some of us are here anew. alhamdullilah!!!

.٣

rise, ya ikhwaan, to the moment,
only won by the prepared,
birthed in struggle,
made bright by hope,

stroked by consistency,
conquered in the heart,
the race that is ramadhan!

RAMADHAN
1443AH

Soul Saum 1

.١

in the name of Allah;

the day starts early
with an eager soul.
in the dead of morning,
distractions at bay,
a welcoming heart;

it is ramadhan.

.٢

the tongue is moist,
the face is wet,
the love for our Lord,
is real and near.

the throat is parched
the sight is stretched
but our smiles are from ear to ear.

.٣

the thirst is quenched
a day well spent
in worship of Allah
alhamdulillah rabbil a'lamin
ramadhan is here.

may Allah grant us
the blessing of our fasts. ameen.

Soul Saum 2

١.

i seek refuge in Allah
from the accursed devil.

'...do you believe in part of the scripture
and disbelieve in part? ...these are the ones
who have bought the life of this world
in exchange for the hereafter' q2 v85 - v86

do you?

٢.

tears:
from punishment
to hard work and reward,
to charity and obedience;
around hypocrisy and through kindness,
in hopelessness, found and firm faith.

٣.

the promise of your Lord
flows through our eyes
and into our hearts
from the top of our bookshelves,
and crevices,
to be immersed in once again
and lived!

.٤

'...our Lord,
indeed we have believed,
so forgive us our sins, and protect
us from the punishment of the fire.

the patient, the true, the obedient, those
who spend (in the way of Allah), those
who seek forgiveness before dawn.' q3 v16 - v17

.٥

hopefully, never to be forgotten.

ya Allah,
may Your admonition and noble words,
soften our souls, and cause us to reflect,
and obey!

this month and always,
ameen.

Soul Saum 3

١.

i am four:

the house is abuzz,
there's food and conversations,
the humm of recitations, and
i love to fast;

i'll eat Iftaar at 9am,
one fast done today!

٢.

i am eight:

why do you fast?
my friends ask

i wonder too

licking my lips hungrily
as their lips shine with oil
my uncles and aunts frown too

٣.

he's too young,
grandma intones.

but i feel my father's glare,

even though he's not there,
i feel it still.

a fast done
today!

.٤

i am eleven:
day three, and i smile;
i made dua at tahajjud today,
i used the miswak before salat,
heading out for taraweeh,
i know why the season.
i know why.

.٥

i look at my sister,
kicking and struggling to suckle;
don't worry little one,
insha Allah,
this mercy will be bestowed
upon you too,

you'll fast one day soon.

.٦

may Allah,
in His infinite mercies,
that encompasses all of creation,
grant us all,
the blessings of this fast,
and of those to come.

ameen.

Soul Saum 4

١.

we work to live,
and live to work,
work and live,
live and work;

as the majority ground out
to a working day today,
did we plan these moments?

٢.

the fleeting distractions?
the unwarranted rhythms?
the conversations
impeding our dhikr?
the frustrations
stretching our limits?
the anger from one another?

٣.

a muslim employer should empathise,
for it's not just payment before sweat dries,
but also the acknowledgement,
that you and your employees
need this time for your Lord.

yes, you!
i am talking to you!

٤.

employers, business owners,
managers, supervisors, muslim;
how is your ramadhan,
and your work life?

for the employer and employee,
your days are an amana from Allah,
so is your sweat.

٥.

it's day four;

it's not too late to be the one,
that changes the grind.

let our days be rahmah for us,
on the day it counts the most.

may Allah accept our ibaadah for His sake.
ameen.

Soul Saum 5

١.

ya ikhwaan!
put your trust in Allah,
and tie your camel.

safety,
first:

for ourselves, at home, at school,
at work, in our environments.

٢.

where are your gas cylinders positioned?
does your stairs have rails?

is there a working fire extinguisher
in your house and car?

do you and your family know how to use it?

do your kids know what to do
in case of an emergency?

٣.

do they know what to do
when confronted in their deen?

wait, what? that line is left-field much
no, it's not.

for as part of emergency training nowadays,
islam and terrorism are banded together
as part of a possible emergency.

٤.

shocked? you should be.
but are they ready?
your household?
you?

be conscious,
be prepared.

learn, teach yourself, and the ummah.

٥.

we need to know
what islam truly teaches,
there's no better time than today.

first, safety:

ya ikhwaan,
tie your camels,
and put your trust in Allah.

Soul Saum 6

١.

abu huraira reported:
the messenger of Allah, pbbuh said,
"gabriel kept advising me
to be good to neighbors
until i thought he would
make them my heirs."
source: sunan ibn mājah 3674

٢.

an admonition to myself first:

do you know the names
of your neighbours
forty houses to your right
and forty houses to your left?

do you?
do you?

٣.

twenty houses?
ten houses?
five?
neighbors next door?
or do we just have greeting acquaintances?

this is not the sunnah of this deen,
awake!

.٤

islam has clothed us
with the best of characters;
our parents greeted all and sundry
on their path to and from home,
much to our chagrin as kids,
and even now,

they seek out the neighbour.

.٥

is this the disapproval that
we have brought into our lives,
and tainted our deen with?

fa audhubillah!

revive,
it's never too late,
it awaits.

.٦

hold your spouse's hand on the right,
and that of your child by the left,
and go make a connection.

revive a sunnah,
up your ibaadah.

may Allah have mercy on our relationships.
ameen. alhamdulillah.

Soul Saum 7

.١

the past is the future,
the future is the past,
tomorrows are actually yesterdays,
and yesterdays are tomorrows;

age is now,
age is timeless,
age is now.

.٢

we live in a continuing circle:
and to truly appreciate our lives,
our time, ourselves, is to reflect
on the past, as it will be our future;

the daughter, the mother,
who will beget a daughter.

a patient, the healer,

.٣

who will be healed;

the scribe, the reader,
who will be written about;

the words,
that will tell your future,
just as it told your past.

.٤

the circle of life is Allah's:
from this world to the next,
different but the same,
the past is the future
the future is the past.

may our circle be enriched in this world
to usher in the best of the next. Ameen

Soul Saum 8

١.

our young adults are
in shaky impetuous times;

changelings,
child not yet an adult,
adult no more a child,
it's a time that most adults
treat with trepidation.

٢.

silent moments we dread to understand,
noisy moments we think are mostly rude,
a delight, a discovery, to have as friends,

an honour.

behind the facade,
a butterfly emerges, one that
loves to be engaged by adults.

٣.

no not necessarily mum and dad,
adults nonetheless.

reach out to one today,
they do cherish your thoughts and time;

for the strength of conviction in your words,
and eyes help build and solidify their dreams,
and their hopes in life.

.٤

abu, ummi;

you have given them wings,
guided them,
now, smile at them,
hug them, and pray.

let them know you're right here,
then, trust them to fly.

.٥

we know they'll never be adults to you,
but, ya ikhwaan,
love our young adults,
for in them you will find you.

and understand, that one day,
they will see you,
and connect.

Soul Saum 9

.١

20/21 days to go, ya ikhwaan,
where are you?

seated making dua?
daydreaming about what to do?
lost in hunger, counting the hours?
walking the streets, smile strained but sweet?

where are you?

.٢

20/21 days, ya ikhwaan,
how have you been?
spent your nights crying to your Lord?
in pain and guilt from the weight of His words?
been in the midst of the needy, the orphan,
been pondering your lot?
how have you been?

.٣

or have you been filling your cup
from the world of books and naseehah?

nine fasts done, those days are gone,
we tighten our belt, each day will be felt,
stronger we strive, with renewed personal drive.

where are you?
how have you been?

.٤

not a competition,
but on a mission
to be better
than we were
the day before,
for the One who is
above us all.

Soul Saum 10

١,

how did this happen
how am i still here?
tired, weary, guilty.

miles done,
but i'm not there,
a spouse, home alone,
but i'm here not there.

٢.

children asleep, without a care,
how, am i here?

toiling, thinking, brainstorming,
supposedly, to please my paymasters,
it's expected of me, it's what i have to do,
it's my job, this i know,
but ya allah; how, am i still here?

٣.

these auspicious days,
in these late hours,
i should be asleep,
or on my knees,
to my benevolent lord,
bringing forth a time

to justify my being

.٤

yet, here i am here,
stuck in the grind of man,
all the things that count,
lying unattended to;

and i, a weak servant, i am,
can only cry; o why?
why am i still here?

.٥

ya Allah,
forgive me,
guide me,
guard me,
help me
move me from here,
to a place that pleases you.

An act of obedience

Abu Atiyyah said:

"Masruq and I entered upon Aishah and we said: 'O Mother of the Believers! There are two men from the Companions of Muhammad, one of them hastens to break the fasts and he hastens to perform Salat. The other delays breaking the fast and he delays the Salat.' She said: 'Which of them hastens to break the fast and hastens to perform the Salat?' We said that it was Abdullah bin Mas'ud. She said: 'This is how the Messenger of Allah did it.' And the other was Abu Musa."

— Jami` at-Tirmidhi 702

Soul Saum 11

١.

ya Rabbi:

bless our work, the sweat of our brow,
the toil of our hands, bless our earnings,
as the sun beats hard on our backs,
our legs trudge down the streets,
our bodies ache from sitting for hours,
put barakah in our strivings. ameen.

٢.

when we leave before the cock crows,
and return to the kids sound asleep;
when quality time is spent closing a deal,
or having a meeting via our handsets;

grant our work meaning, so this 'busy-ness',
does not endanger our relationship with You,
our spouses, children, family, and friends.

٣.

ya Allah:

purify our deeds,

rectify our intentions,
cleanse our dealings,
make our work count for us,
not against us now,

and in the life to come. ameen.

*the second stretch has begun, may Allah
make us witnesses to His mercy. ameen.*

Soul Saum 12

١.

broken homes,
our children are not to be blamed
for our mistakes, our anger, our frustrations;
our children need love, attention, and guidance.

most of them act up looking for these,
and in the process may even get abused,
parents, be alert.

٢.

your child's attitude cannot be fixed
by your shouting, further negligence or insults;
tough love is not supposed to destroy
the esteem of your child, make them fear you,
or make them hate you.

o parents!
they are an amana from Him to you.

٣.

no matter the circumstances
between you both,
hold tight,
to your covenant
with Allah
through them;

hold tight.

.٤

ya ikhwaan!

somewhere around you
is a child from such a home;

do not turn away from them,
be the comfort, be the benefit,
be the mumin be the muslim;

do not turn away.

Soul Saum 13

.١

people are beautiful,
in their different flavours,
and characters:

the happy and vibrant, the sad but hopeful,
the young and loud, the shy and misunderstood,
the harsh and uncouth; everybody has a colour
that makes up this kaleidoscope called life.

.٢

the ummah is especially calming;
have you not felt the strength of the salam?

a sister's smile at another
across a crowded hall,
a brother's hug before boarding a bus;

all united on one thing,
their belief in Allah.

.٣

another thing that springs
from our flavours is communication;

in speech or action, it
makes this bond complete.

so, beautify your manners,
ya akhii, ya ukhtii,
smile.

٤.

make seventy excuses for your brother,
do not be suspicious of one another;

want for the other,
what you love for yourself;

be brethren ya ikhwaan.

a wonderful people of musk you are.
alhamdulillah.

Soul Saum 14

١.

salvation and true success
lies in the purification
of the heart;

for Allah said
in q91 v9:

*qad aflha
man zakkaha.*

٢.

and it is in the
remembrance of Allah
that hearts find rest;

for Allah said
in q13 v28:

*ala bi dhikrillahi
tatmainnul qulub.*

٣.

achievement is by grace of Allah,
and not by any merit of yours;

for Allah said
in q3 v37:

innallaha yarzuqu manyashaau
bi gayri hisab.

be mindful.

.٤

remember all these,
and you will avoid pride;

to hold on to Allah,
you must be grateful,
worship and love Him,
become His hanif and
make jihad for Him.

.٥

but to implement these
you must shun pride,
hypocrisy, pessimism;
you must control your anger,
your lustful sexual passion;
watch your tongue,
eyes, ears, limbs;

.٦

your mission is to perform da'wah,
preserve your islamic identity,
teach the youth and live by the example
of the prophet, sallalahu alayhi wa salam.

do not covet this world, and Allah will love you;

do not covet what people possess,
and the people will love you.

.٧

repel evil,
with that which is better;

be merciful,
to the people in this world;

so that the One above may be merciful to you;
forgive, have patience,
and persevere.

.٨

your brother must be able to count on you
in their moments of need, adversity, and
in their moments of prosperity too -
that you won't wish that they lose
that which they just prospered in,
that you will support them, and
not make them feel alone.

.٩

preparation to meet Allah
must be the purpose and
ultimate goal of our existence;

the knowledge that Allah is pleased
with us should be the climax of our life mission;

for islam is a state of becoming,
not a state of being.

Soul Saum 15

.١

the muslim will have two joys:

when he breaks his fast,
and when he meets his Lord
because of his fast;

the joys of breaking the fast.

the joys of preserving,
and disciplining the soul.

.٢

you are fulfilled,
another day done;

the aromas from the kitchen,
meets the thirst from your tongue,
finally, all come into harmony;

and it is ibaadah,
a path to Allah.

.٣

now, breaking the fast
in community?

an added benefit on our scales,
and for each other; as Allah,
in His glorious book, assures us
of the barakah of feeding one another;

so, share the joys of the fast.

٤.

make dua to Allah
for providing for us, when
so many do not have;

tomorrow, we go again,
eager to please our Lord
but tonight, alhamdullilah
for the fast.

٥.

it's the halfway mark ya ikhwaan,
alhamdulillah.

take stock,
plan, prepare
and act!

alhamdulillah,
alhamdulillah rabil a'lamin.

A gift as we enter the half way mark from Sofiyat Popoola-
CEO Konnoisseur Konsult

Reflections from Surat Zumar.

Do not despair of His Mercy

Feeling like an outcast and looking so downcast,
As the depth of your sin,
Chases you to the bin.
Making you feel useless and stopping you from caring,
Because they are indeed alarming.

Stop!
It's time to re-write your story. Insha Allah, in the end, it will
be full of glory.
The Most High detests seeing you shabby,
Carrying worries around and moving like a loaded donkey

He accepts sincere tawbah
As far as it comes with deep remorse.
So, turn to Him and find repose.
So much wrong you do against your soul,
Fellow souls and to the Owner of it all.

You think heaven's door has been slammed against you.
Envisaging your voice too faint to be heard by The One who
made you.
There is glad tiding if you are sincere.
And Verse 53 of this chapter is one of such reference

So, soak yourself in the cloak of regret,
Seek istigfar as much as the forgiveness you hope to get.

Don't return to old habits.
Even if it lays rampant in the streets.

Do not despair of the mercy of Your Lord.

Jazakallahu Khairan for sharing your words Sis

Soul Saum 16

.١

this is for you:

for holding us,
together;
through sweat and sleet,
in the rain or heat,
in emotional or financial adversity
you stand tall, this is for you.

.٢

this is for you:

for engaging all,
young and old,
for helping in the kitchen,
stitching your clothes,
in patience - holding soft,
but strong, this is for you.

.٣

this is for you:

for your silent approvals,
or disapprovals; for your love,
protection, mistakes, stumbling,
weaknesses, and everything in between.

for being vulnerable, yet unbroken,
this is for you.

٤.

this is for you:

we see, we know,
we understand;

for being the standard, the unique
for not being like any other, but
the best of you amongst all men.

this is for you.

٥.

this is for you:

sons, brothers, husbands
fathers, uncles, grandfathers,
the men in our lives.

this is for you,
may Allah increase you in eeman,
hikmah and sabr. ameen.

Soul Saum 17

١.

and it began, the build-up, the anger,
from the depth of your stomach
curling your toes, firing up your brain.

'couldn't she get anything right?'
'what's wrong with him?'
'why did he speak to me like that?'
'how could she just walk out on me?'

٢.

it's churning, sickening, you struggle,
to bring the thought to your head,

'i am fasting, i am fasting, i am fasting',

furiously, you turn away,
move away, stay away.

be calm, control yourself,
you are summoned.

٣.

scolded for not having control,
reminded, you baulk, chastised;
the pit in your stomach raw, but fading.

they are muslims, fasting;
'why didn't he take care
of how he behaved?'
'why was she so rude?'

.٤

you sit,
you breathe,
calmer now;

you whisper,
ya Allah forgive me,
ya Allah, still grant me
the blessings of this day.

.٥

then,
i make dua for me,
i make dua for him,
i make dua for her;

'we are fasting,
we are fasting',
alhamdullilah.

Soul Saum 18

.١

i struggle:

the sound of the worship house down the road
whose basals have no care for its surroundings,
surround my head from all corners;

i raise my voice in desperation, to drown
out the repeated chorus that's becoming
horribly familiar to the drums in my ears.

.٢

i struggle:

the door creaks open
as they tumble into the room
with no care in the world;

their noise is accompanied
by the shrill cries
of the little one.

.٣

i struggle:

now, gasps and loud whispers
echo as everyone attempts

a semblance of quietude;
i almost let out an audible sigh,
serenity stolen from me
as I struggle.

.٤

i clear my thoughts
and bring forth
my last day

i perform my wudhu
in fear, i don't know the lines
but i recite, inspired, knowing
the One i pray to and why;

.٥

the sounds fade away,
and the tears brim and fall,
as i call to my Lord
the struggle is on;

ya Allah, grant us khushuoo in our salat
forgive our shortcomings and
purify our ibaadah. amin.

Soul Saum 19

.١

today is a good day,
now is a good time;
make the most of your hours,
for every moment is precious:

that call you've been meaning
to make,
make it.

.٢

today is a good day,
now is a good time;
your hours are what you make of it,
your life is how you choose;
that book you want to write
put pen to paper,
and write.

.٣

today is a good day,
now is a good time;

that person you're afraid
to talk to, talk to them
that idea you can't get
out of your head,
get up and try it out.

.٤

today is a good day,

now is a good time,
the perfect time;

your tomorrow
starts with now
if you're still preparing,
you'll be too late.

٥.

today is a good day,
now is a good time;

with your heart beating and unsure,
your thoughts wavering,
now is the time.
the quran you've been meaning to learn.
memorize, start with a verse.

٦.

today is a good day,
now is a good time;
the duas you keep
forgetting to say,
part your lips.

the last ten are upon us.
it is not too late.

٧.

today is a good day,
now is a good time;
today, now,
now is a good time,
today is a good day;

start,
now...

Soul Saum 20

.١

don't get carried away,
Allah has blessed you,
with a good home, job, business,
some relative success,
peace, comfort,
joy, sustenance;

alhamdulillah.

.٢

don't get carried away,
Allah has made charity easy for you,
you give before you have,
you've completed the quran in ramadhan,
you have the love of the people,
knowledge has been made easy for you;

alhamdulillah.

.٣

don't get carried away,
you were in hardship, and
the Most Merciful granted you ease;
you suddenly are well known,
your words are listened to
across the globe;

alhamdulillah.

.٤

don't get carried away,
you my akhii, you my ukhtii,
remember who you are
remember why you are here
servant! worshipper!
remember,
do not forget;

.٥

and if there is anything
you say, write, live that
does not reflect this, then,
you have no idea
who you are;
think,
reflect.

.٦

how are you proud?
boastful and ungrateful?
o muslim!

your words, your pride, your gratitude;
on your sense of becoming,
it's the last ten!

don't get carried away

*may Allah make it easy for us
as we strive hard from tonight. ameen.*

As a protection

Narrated Abu Huraira:

Allah's Messenger (ﷺ) said, "Fasting is a shield. [So, the one fasting should practice] no intimacy and no foolishness, and if a man fights with him or insults him, he should tell him twice, 'I am fasting'."

"By Him in Whose Hands my soul is, the mouth odour of a fasting person is better in the sight of Allaah than the smell of musk. [Allaah says about the fasting person], 'He leaves his food, drink and desires for My sake.

The fast is for Me, and it is I Who rewards it, and a good deed is [rewarded] with ten of its like."

— Sahih al-Bukhari 1894

Soul Saum 21

.١

it's the ten,
the last ten days,
of ramadhan:

for the new day that you rise
into the life, you did not create;
ibadillah, will you not be grateful?

it's the ten.

.٢

compare your life
to that of the family
that can barely feed itself,
or those that live at the mercy
of Allah's winds, where schools
are a mirage for their kids;

compare your life, ibadillah.

.٣

compare your life
to those that good health
and mind has been taken
as a trial from our Lord;

ibadillah, should you not weep?
should you not think?
should you not wake?

٤

what did you do
to be so wealthy?
to speak so eloquently?
to be so revered?
to be so clever?
to be so honoured?
to be so loved?

٥.

what did you do
to be so hardworking?
to be so patient?
to be so entrepreneurial?

what did you do, ibadillah?

to have everything
you've ever wanted?

٦.

ibadillah!

do you think it's because
of something you did?

have you spared a thought
for the One who decided this will be?

you?
it's the last ten, ya ibadillah.

.٧

as you prepare that long list of askings,
prepare an even longer list of gratitude,
for witnessing these days,
for being in good health,
for being in good state of mind,
for being;

for being muslim.

.٨

and,
know,
ibadillah,
that one cannot show
enough gratitude
to one's Creator.

alhamdullilah.

Soul Saum 22

١.

give a little of yourself,
cure your greed,
purify your wealth;

look around you,
where you live,
work, play, shop,
look around you:

٢.

look at all the good
you have to give,
give a little of yourself.
every joint of man
is enjoined to give
wealth every day;

give a little of yourself.

٣.

remove something harmful from the road
help one another by wealth, by naseehah,
by saying a kind word, by giving a smile;

it is all charity.

give a little of yourself,
despite your love for it,
give anyway.

٤.

knowing you are giving
not for the sake
of the one receiving
but giving for Allah's sight alone;
so that it may count for you
in this world and the next;

this is charity.

٥.

that spending that we do not cloud
and beautify for the whole world
to picture and praise one for;
that spending that the left hand
cannot see what the right hand
gave even if it it stretched its limbs;

this is charity.

٦.

that spending that you give
solely for His sake alone,
purely, quietly, intently,
in obedience, for qiyammah;

this is charity.

may Allah make it easy for us
to give without fear of want. ameen.

Soul Saum 23

.١

it's the last ten days,
six or seven days to go;

and, i lied,
it was ten minutes after eight,
i should have said,
'i was late',
instead, i said the kids were the reason.

.٢

yes, i lied,
a phone call for business,
another from family,
i ignore one
for the other,
and explain very quickly,
'sorry, someone was using my phone'.

.٣

yes, i lied,
some monies are needed,
i'll pay back they promise
but to this you doubt
just to keep the ties,
'sorry,
really tight'

.٤

yes, i lied,
when i said i didn't know it was broken, i lied;
when i said i wasn't going to leave the young
one alone, but snuck out afterwards, i lied;
when i said i was weak, when actually,
i was strong, i lied; when i said i was there,
when i was truly here, i lied; o how we lie.

.٥

yet, in this blessed month of ours
what's a fast with a lie?
Allah has no need of the fast
of one who lies.

ya Allah
purify our thoughts, and deeds.
forgive us when we lie.

Soul Saum 24

.١

make dua
for someone
in your long list
remember the stranger
who shielded you
from the mischief
of the road

.٢

make dua
for the sister
who paid
for you
at the counter
because she noticed
you were straitened

.٣

make dua
for your parents
who raised you
in islam
through doubt and struggle
in faith and hope
wanting akhirah alone

.٤

make dua
for your siblings
who you fight endlessly

as regards the deen
trying to keep the ties of kin
pulling away but
pushing forth

.٥

make dua
for you friends
who held you
when you were low
or stumbling to find their way
or admonished you
when you strayed

.٦

make dua
for family
near and far
make dua
for your acquaintances
who ridicule
and mock

.٧

make dua
for the ummah, for oppressed,
for those in need - of a spouse,
of children - for wherewithal,
for barakah,
for peace of mind
make dua.

and may the angels say
'amin, and to you too'.

Soul Saum 25

.١

it's the last five
from the last ten;

be conscious
be consistent,
be inspired,
be the servant,
be muslim;

.٢

when the next driver yells an obscenity, call to
account that it is for al Fattah that you react;

when you rise at night to follow the jammah,
call to account that it is for your Rabb's sight you aim;

when you make the meals and wash
the dishes, call to account that it is for your Lord
that you serve your family and friends;

.٣

when you listen to your parents against your judgement,
call to account ar Rahman,
for it is Him you obey;

when you dash out to work instead of being in the 'mode'
these last days,
these last days,
call to account Allah,
as it is ibaadah for you - to work, and not beg,

٤.

know this, ya ikhwaan;
that consciously putting thought
into everything we do
makes our whole life and living,
worship.

may Allah accept our ibaadah as the last
days in this beloved month roll out. amin.

Soul Saum 26

.١

the destroyer of dreams, plans and fantasies,
the tumbler that will pass over each one of us,
the one event that is certain for us without fail,
no one returns
to prepare you,
no one returns
to tell you of its stories;

.٢

for some,
this door is the end,
an end to the troubles
of this life's fleetingness;

so there's nothing
to fear
except the door

.٣

to others, for us;
it's what's behind the door
that we fear.

what have we sent forth?
deeds that will give us emerald cushions
and silk, or deeds that will give blazing embers

of regret, unending, unrelaxed.

٤.

the sahabah before us
never feared the door,
for they worked for it tirelessly,
and so should we.

they laughed little,
wept more, and
so should we.

٥.

death should be a door to our beginning,
not the end.

may Allah make us amongst those
that their souls will be slipped
from their bodies, shrouded in perfumes,
and given glad tidings of jannah.

amin.

Soul Saum 27

.١

to attain happiness, first, know this,
that the past is gone,
that the future is yet to come
but that today is yours.

leave your mistakes
and worries in the past,
you cannot rewind time.

.٢

the future is the world of the unseen
some of us won't make it.

but today, right now,
own it! do it all!
now!
be nice, be kind,
but expect no thanks.

.٣

don't trouble yourself with criticism,
kindness is the musk of the believer,
your frown never availed anyone,
not even you, do it for Allah;

you are unique,

there's only one of you,

be you, everyone else is taken;

٤.

ponder and give thanks,
think of the favour of your Rabb,
and use your spare time to work,
worship, read, and beware of an idle mind.

know, that what was meant for you,
will never miss you, and what has missed you,
was never meant for you.

٥.

do your all,
but in the end,
it is as it should be.

the pen
is lifted,
and the ink
is dried.

Soul Saum 28

.١

to attain happiness:

know that,
eeman is living.

the believer knows that
it's in the remembrance of Allah,
that the heart finds rest,
so, he calls to Him.

.٢

his situation is always good,
for in joy and pleasure, in distress,
or in need of succour,
he says 'alhamdullilah',
he knows recompense is with Allah
and behind every cloud, is a silver lining;
for verily with hardship, comes ease.

.٣

so he is patient,
and expectant of good from his Lord.
he stays away from the people and places
that do not remind him of this.

surround yourself with people

and gatherings of benefit

if not, stay in your homes!

.٤

the believer is gentle, yet purposeful,
gets benefit from the flower,
without crushing it;

makes lemonade out of lemons.

indeed, he is the date palm tree,
a benefit and a blessing
to all.

.٥

o mumin,
beware of envy,
do not let it creep in,
do not let it creep into your heart;
do not question your Creator
by being envious
of someone that has what you long for.

.٦

face life as it is,
its good times,
and bad ones;
this world is a trial for you.

eeman is life by Allah
for Allah, and with Allah.
alhamdullilah.

Soul Saum 29

.١

my body aches, my soul cries,
how has the time gone yet again?

in business and contemplation,
neighbours, children, charity, safety,
time, learning, men, beauty, truth,
worship, reading, dua, forgiveness,
muslim, the ummah, on our Lord

.٢

so many lessons, and
so many things to be thankful for;
oh, how the time ran by.

it's up to us, to keep time here,
the shaytan and shayateen,
cannot beat a prepared slave;
burnt gold from the heat of ramadhan.

.٣

life will try to take over,
seclusions will end,
the kids will need tending to,
our needs must be met;
my dearest ones, hold on,
for with striving in 29

we are emboldened for 365.

٤.

believe,
have faith,
work!
with just a step,
then two,
the time is now.
we will miss ramadhan!

Soul Saum 30

.١

in attaining happiness, know that,
it is of this life to experience trials,
take consolation from the stricken;
for you who is sick is the dying one;
for you struggling is one derelict;
there will always be someone worse,
until we reach the grave.

.٢

so take consolation, for Allah is sufficient for us,
and is the best disposer of our affairs.

seek help and patience in the prayer,
for the one who abandons the prayer
has lost the tranquillity for the soul;

in sorrow, pain or happiness,
the prayer, the prayer, the prayer.

.٣

guard strictly your salat,
and have beautiful patience,
travel and marvel, at the bounties
of your Lord, call the adhan in the mountains,
extol His glory amongst the trees, and let the
wind and rain lift you; do not carry the weight

of the world on your shoulders, do not.

٤.

do not be ignited by the pettiness, and
fleetingness of this life; your worries will
always be heavier than it truly is.

so be content with what you have
been bestowed by your Lord,
for your provision will suffice you.

yes, it will.

٥.

o just nation!
striving for the middle course!

with the goal in sight,
of the place in the heavens
that no eyes have ever seen,
or mind comprehended;

alhamdullilah.

Shawwal

.١

and,
i return,
or attempt to,
and i fail,
again, and
yet again;
i fail.

.٢

the pull of the dunya is real, ya ikhwaan,
i ask myself, why? despite my best efforts;

my head is willing, my heart is willing,
but why does my actions still fail me?

i try to make dua, but i drift, i drift to the last
conversation i had, the last image i looked upon,
the last chore i engaged in, i drift, yes, i drift.

.٣

in the pauses of frustration, i realise why,
for you cannot want, without action;

you cannot bathe in the waters of eeman,
whirl in the dust of jahannam, and then
hope for a miraculous outcome.

you cannot have the frivolities of this world,
and want or earn the gems of the hereafter.

٤.

is it not for this
that we are warned
to surround ourselves
with halal and unharmful?

food, drink, company, leisure,
earnings, if it's tainted, then the
journey to return will always fail.

٥.

so, start simple;

leave the late night eating,
that makes you too full
to recite your night dua,
leave the entertainment
that befuddles your mind,
and makes morning engagement with your Lord.

٦.

say goodbye to the ones who glamorise the lifestyle
you are in doubt of, and are trying to leave behind.

engage in less conversation
away from the memories of your Rabb,
plan your day, and truly engage your Rabb,
learn about Him anew, and all over again;
read about the Prophet pbuh anew, and all over again;

٧.

be inspired
by the righteous ones,
anew and all over again;
recite, listen, and understand
the Quran anew and all over again;

return,
a little at a time.

٨.

give naseehah
and in turn, give yourself,
step away, walk away, remember.
you must leave before you can return,
return, ya ikhwaan,
return to Allah,
peace.

May Allah grant us the blessings of our fasts a thousandfold, by His Mercy! Ameen.

Ya Allah, all praise and worship is to You for this gift to pen words of remembrance which You found it worthy to bestow on Your slave. Ya Allah may I earn Your pleasure because of this. Ameen.

* 9 7 9 8 4 3 3 2 6 0 4 7 4 *